YOUTH FICTION

# Time to Talk

**Iris Howden**

*Published in association with*
The Basic Skills Agency

Hodder & Stoughton

A MEMBER OF THE HODDER HEADLINE GROUP

**Acknowledgements**
*Illustrations: Mike Bell/Ian Fleming Associates.*
*Cover: Stuart Williams/Organisation.*

Orders: please contact Bookpoint Ltd, 39 Milton Park, Abingdon, Oxon OX14 4TD. Telephone: (44) 01235 400414, Fax: (44) 01235 400454. Lines are open from 9.00–6.00, Monday to Saturday, with a 24 hour message answering service. Email address: orders@bookpoint.co.uk

ISBN 0 340 72093 X

First published 1998
Impression number 10 9 8 7 6 5 4 3 2
Year 2001 2000 1999



Typeset by Fakenham Photosetting Ltd, Fakenham, Norfolk.
Printed in Great Britain for Hodder & Stoughton Educational, a division of Hodder Headline Plc, 338 Euston Road, London NW1 3BH by Athenaeum Press Ltd, Gateshead, Tyne & Wear.

# Time to Talk

## Contents

# 1

# Bad News

Kate was in the bathroom washing her hair.
The door bell rang.
She grabbed a towel.
Put it round her wet hair.
'Hang on,' she shouted. 'I'm coming.'

A policeman stood on the door step.
It was Jeff Barnes.
Kate knew him well.
He worked with her brother, Andy.
Andy was a policeman too.
'Hi, Jeff,' she began to say.
But Jeff looked very serious.
'Come inside,' he said. 'Sit down.
It's bad news, I'm afraid.'

Jeff rang Kate's sister-in-law Jane.
She said she'd come over.
Kate sat on the sofa
numb with shock.
She looked round the room.
At the cards on the side-board.
GOOD LUCK ON YOUR WEDDING DAY,
they said.
She looked at the pile of presents
on the table.

Glasses and dishes. Pots and pans.
Sheets and towels.
A toaster, a kettle, an iron.
They'd all have to be sent back.

Kate went upstairs in a daze.
She began to dry her hair.
Her white wedding dress hung
like a sad ghost behind the door.
Her white veil lay over a chair.
Her white satin shoes under it.
She would never wear them now.
There would be no wedding.
Gary was dead.

Andy and his wife Jane took over.
They were very kind.
She went to stay at their house for a while.
They helped her pack up the presents.
They rang family and friends.
Told them about the accident.

Andy went to cancel the church.
To cancel the wedding meal.
To cancel the cars and flowers.
Jane took the wedding dress back to the shop.

A few days later they all met in church.
But not for a wedding.
This time it was for Gary's funeral.
With Jane and Andy's help,
Kate got through the day.
It was the worst day of her life.

# 2

# A New Friend

After a few days Kate began to make plans.
She wanted to keep the house.
The house she and Gary had saved for.
But her wage wouldn't cover the mortgage.
'I'll get someone in to share,' she told Andy.
'Help pay the bills.'

'Well choose someone quiet,' Andy said.
'Someone you can rely on.
Who'll pay the rent on time.
A non smoker with no children or pets.'
Kate put an advert in the paper.
She put one in the corner shop window.

A lot of people came to look at the room.
'I'll let you know,' Kate told them all.
She couldn't bear to think of any of them
living in her house. Sitting at her table.
Sleeping in the room she had planned
to share with Gary.

Then Fran turned up.
She didn't look at all quiet.
Fran was black. She was big and jolly.
She talked non-stop in a loud voice.
And she laughed a lot.

Fran was an art student.
Her clothes were all the colours of the rainbow.
She wore huge gold ear-rings.

She picked up Gary's photo.
'Was this your boyfriend?' she asked.
'He looks a nice guy. Full of life.'
She stopped. 'I'm sorry,' she said.
'That was a really stupid thing to say.'
'No,' Kate said. 'It's OK. You're right.
Gary was full of life.
He was always laughing and joking.
Always on the go.'

'What happened?' Fran asked.
'It was a road accident,' Kate said.
'He was on his motor bike.
Going too fast as usual.
He loved going fast.'
It was good to talk about it.
Since his death no-one had spoken
Gary's name.
Her friends all changed the subject if Kate
talked about him.
Fran was the only person who
had been at ease.
Kate liked her for it.
Fran was a warm person.
She was good fun.
She would cheer the place up.
'When can you move in?' Kate said.

# 3

# Back to Work

Kate went back to work.
She worked as a nurse.
It was hard at first.
No-one knew what to say to her.
They all felt sorry for her.
Kate should have been on her honeymoon.
Instead, she had been to Gary's funeral.
She looked pale and thin.

'Are you sure you're up to this?'
Sister Moore asked. 'We're very busy.
Half the staff are off with flu.'

The ward was full.
Even the small private room at the end
was being used.
A policeman sat outside it on a chair.
'What's going on?' Kate asked the Sister.
'A young man was stabbed,' she said.
'There was a fight in a squat in town.
About drugs. A girl died of an over-dose.
He's in a bad way.
The police want to question him.'
Next day Andy was there on duty.
Kate took him a cup of tea.
'He's out cold,' he told Kate.
'Still not able to talk.
It makes me mad having to waste time
on scum like him.'
Kate went into the room.
She read the chart at the foot of the bed.
The patient's name was Nick Clark.

'Well, Nick Clark,' she said softly.
'You've been lucky.'
The knife blade had just missed his heart.
Kate thought how unfair life was.
That Nick had lived while Gary had died.

When Nick came round, Andy spoke to him.
He asked him questions about the fight.
On his way out he looked in
at the nurses' office.
'I'm off, Sis,' he said. 'I'll be seeing you.
Jane wants you to come round for a meal
soon.'
'Thanks,' Kate said. She smiled.

Andy was still her big brother.
He looked after her.
Just as he had when they were at school.

Later, she went in to give Nick his medicine.
He was wide awake.
He lay staring up at the ceiling.
'How are you feeling?' she asked.
Nick didn't answer.
He turned his head away.
None of the nurses liked him.
He wouldn't speak to anyone.

Kate was a good nurse.
Nick was still her patient.
– whatever he had done.
'Let me make you more comfortable,'
she said.
She smoothed out the top sheet.
Plumped up the pillow on his bed.

'Do you need anything?' she asked.
'A drink? A pain-killer to help you sleep?'
Nick shook his head.
Kate knew that the pain
wasn't just in his ribs.
She saw that the hurt was deep inside.

In the morning she was sent to wash him.
Nick pushed her hand away.
He kicked the bowl of water off the bed.
It spilled all over the floor.
Kate mopped it up.
She did not say anything.
She left Nick alone.
Lying with his face to the wall.
Kate knew how he felt.
She had been there herself.

# 4

# A Meeting in the Park

Months passed.
Kate got on with her life.
Work kept her busy. She was glad
she had Fran to go home to.
There was always reggae music playing.
A good smell of food in the kitchen.

Fran cooked Caribbean dishes.
Fish stew, peas and rice, spicy chicken.
'I should do my share of the cooking,'
Kate told Fran.
'No way,' Fran said. 'I enjoy it.
Besides, your cooking's rubbish!'
Kate laughed. Fran always spoke her mind.

Andy and Jane were kind to her too.
Kate often went over to their house.
Sometimes Jeff was there.
Kate was sure Andy was trying
to match-make.
Get them to go out together.
'It's too soon,' she told Fran.
'I'm not ready to date anyone yet.'
'Then tell Andy that,' Fran said.
'It's time you stood up to your brother.
You're not a kid any more.'

One Sunday, Kate was at a loose end.
Fran was out with her friends.
Andy and Jane were on holiday.
A long empty day lay ahead.
Outside, the sun was shining.
It was much too nice to stay indoors.
Kate packed some sandwiches and a drink.
She put the Sunday paper in her bag.
She walked to the park.

It was May time.
The trees were in new leaf.
The water of the lake shone like silver
in the sun.
Kate sat down on a bench.
She saw a young man working
on the flower beds.
Kate thought she knew him.
She looked again. It was Nick Clark.

He saw her and came over.
'Hi,' he said. 'It's Kate, isn't it?'
'How are you?'
'I'm fine,' she said. 'How are you?'
Nick looked much better.
He was not so thin now.
He had a tan from working outside.
And he was smiling.
Kate thought how good looking he was.

'I'm doing OK' Nick said.
'Sorting my life out. Listen,
that time – when I was in hospital.
Things were bad. I was very low.
I'm sorry if I gave you a hard time.'
'That's OK' Kate said. 'You were ill.'
'No, it was more than that,' Nick said.
'And you were always so kind.
It can't have been easy for you.'

'I heard the others talking –
about the accident.
I just wanted to say how sorry I was.'

'I'm getting over it,' Kate said.
'But tell me about yourself.
Do you like this job?'
'It's fine for the time being,' Nick said.
'I don't want to do it for ever.
But I'm back on track now.
Getting a flat and so on.
I'm doing odd jobs as well.
Trying to get some money together.'

'Our garden's a mess,' Kate said.
'We never have time to do it.
I'll give you our phone number.'
'Great,' Nick said. 'I'll be in touch.'

As she walked home Kate began to wonder.
Had she done the right thing
– asking Nick to call?
Andy didn't think so.
'You must be mad!' he said.
'Bringing that lay-about to the house.'

'There's no harm in giving the guy
a chance,' Fran said. 'People change.'
'Maybe,' Andy said.
'Don't say I didn't warn you!'

# 5

# The Break-in

A few weeks later it seemed as if Andy might be right.
Nick had been to do the garden that day.
It looked good.
The lawn was smooth and green.
The flower beds were neat.

'You have to admit he's done a great job,'
Kate told her brother when he called.
'Do you want a coffee?'
She went into the kitchen.

A minute later Andy heard her cry out.
'What's the matter?' he asked.
Kate pointed to an empty sweet tin.
The lid lay on the work top.
'Our house-keeping money's gone,'
she told Andy.
'There was a week's shopping money
in that tin.'
'Don't tell me you girls keep money
lying around the house,' Andy said.
'Hang on. Didn't you say that
Nick Clark was here today?
I don't think we need look any further.'

'I can't believe Nick would rob us,'
Kate said.
'His sort never change,' Andy told her.
'I'll go round to his place now.'

Just at that moment Fran came in.
She was loaded with shopping.
She dumped the bags on the kitchen table.
'That's better,' she said. 'My arms
were just about to drop off.'
She looked from their faces to the tin
in Andy's hand. 'It's OK' she told them.
'We haven't been robbed.
My friend Pam had the car today.
We stocked up at the supermarket.'
She fished in her bag.
'Here's the change,' she told Kate.
She dropped some coins into the tin.

Only days later they had a real break-in.
Kate came home to find the kitchen door open.
There was broken glass on the floor.
She saw at once that the microwave had gone.
She went into the living room.
The TV and video were missing.
Upstairs, her bedroom was in a mess.
Drawers were out, clothes flung about.
The wardrobe door hung open.
She looked in her jewellery box.
Her gold watch was gone.
The thief had also taken her camera.

Fran's room was just the same.
What upset her most was the loss
of her computer.
'My college work was on the disc,'
she told Kate.
'I'll have to do it all again.'

She began to cry.
Kate had never seen Fran so down.
'Don't cry,' she told her friend.
'I'll ring Andy. He'll get things moving.'

The police came round.
They took fingerprints.
'Don't worry,' Andy said.
'Your stuff's marked.
We'll soon get it back.'
He had an odd look on his face.
The next day Nick Clark was arrested.
Kate was angry.
She didn't believe Nick had done it.
'You've got it in for Nick,' she told Andy.
'Don't forget. You were wrong
about the money.'
'Face it, Sis,' Andy said. 'Clark's prints
are all over Fran's table.
He's our thief alright.'

Then they had a call from the police.
Two lads had been into a second-hand shop
trying to sell the girls' TV set.
The shop-keeper had rung the police.
'I knew it wasn't Nick,' Kate told Fran.
'How come his prints were on your table?'
'He helped me carry it upstairs,' Fran said.
'I forgot all about it until now.
Talk about give a dog a bad name!
Your brother really hates Nick.'
'Let's hope he sees sense now,' Kate said.
She wanted Andy to like Nick.
She thought he was really nice.

# 6

# The Party

After that they saw a lot of Nick.
He still did the garden but he often
just popped in for a chat.
He and Fran got on well.
They spent hours together
working on her computer.

'Fran's got some great programs,' Nick said.
'She's teaching me to use them.'
'The guy's got talent,' Fran told Kate.

Kate was pleased for Nick but she felt
left out. He and Fran seemed so close.
She was short with him one time.
She'd been left alone all evening.
'What's wrong?' Nick asked.
'Have I upset you?'
'Of course not!' Kate snapped.
'I'm just tired. I work hard for a living.
I can't stay up playing stupid games.
I'm off to bed. Goodnight.'

Then Nick got his own flat.
He and Fran were round there a lot.
Kate felt hurt that he hadn't asked her too.
But a week later he handed her an envelope.

'What's this?' she asked.
'An invitation to my flat-warming party.'
Kate opened the envelope.
Inside was a printed invitation card.
'What do you think?' Nick asked.
'It's all my own work.'
The design on it was really good.
'It's fantastic,' Kate said.
'Fran's right. You do have talent.'

'There's one here for Andy and Jane,'
Nick said.
'You're inviting Andy?' Kate was surprised.
'After the way he's treated you?'
'Live and let live,' Nick said.
'I don't blame him.
He was only looking after you.
Families should stick together.'
'How about you?' Kate asked.

'Have you any family?'
Nick didn't answer.
He looked at his watch.
'Is that the time? I must go.
See you on Saturday. Bye.'

There was quite a crowd at the party.
Kate went from room to room.
'The flat looks great,' she told Nick.
'Thanks to Fran. She helped me fix it.'
'Are those all your own designs?' Kate asked.
She pointed to the posters on the walls.
'Yes,' Nick said. 'Fran's helped me
get a folder of my work together.
I'm going to apply for art college.'

'They're terrific,' Jane said
coming up to join them.
'Don't you think so, Andy?'
'Yes, great,' Andy said. 'First class.'

Kate was taken aback to hear Andy admit it.
'I see you paint people as well,' Jane said.
She pointed to a painting over the fire-place.
It was of a very pretty girl.
'Not really,' Nick said. 'That's a one-off.
She was someone very special to me.'
He moved away from them.
'That's the girl who died in the squat,'
Andy said. 'I'd know her anywhere.'
Kate felt herself go cold.
The girl must have been his girlfriend.
That's why he'd been so upset in hospital.
She had been a fool.
Letting herself fall for him.
There was no way Nick thought of her
that way. He still hadn't got over it.
Kate made an excuse and went home early.

Next morning Fran looked the worse for wear.
'That was some party,' she told Kate.
'What happened? Why did you leave so early?'
'I had a headache,' Kate lied.
'Did you see Nick's designs?' Fran went on.
'Weren't they great?'
'Yes,' Kate said. 'And the painting.
Who was that girl?' she asked,
trying to sound casual. 'His girlfriend?'

'That was his sister,' Fran said. 'She died.
She was only 17. Nick looked after her,
after their mum died. Susie went a bit wild.
She got in with a bad crowd.
Then she went to live in a squat.
Nick moved in as well to keep an eye on her.
Susie got this boyfriend who was a pusher.
She started doing drugs.
He gave her some bad dope and she died.
When Nick found out, they had a fight.
That's when he got stabbed.'

'I think he's done really well to turn
his life around.
Even your Andy said so last night.
That's why I was glad to help him.'
'I feel like a fool,' Kate said.
'I was jealous. I thought you and he . . .'
'Were an item?' Fran laughed.
'I should be so lucky! Anyone can see
he's only got eyes for you, Kate.'

'But . . .' Kate said. 'He's never said anything.'
'That may be my fault,' Fran said.
'He told me ages ago he was keen on you.
But I told him what you said about Jeff.
That it was too soon.'
'That was months ago,' Kate said.
'Besides, I didn't fancy Jeff.'

'And you do fancy Nick?'
Kate nodded.
'I never thought that I could love
anyone after Gary.
But I really like Nick –
he is a good friend,
and maybe, in time . . .'
'Well, don't tell me, tell him,' Fran said.
'Now's your chance.'

They looked out of the window.
Nick was coming up the path.
The door bell rang.
'I'll leave you to it,' Fran said.
'I've got plenty to do.'
Kate went to answer the door.
Nick stood there looking shy.
'Come in,' Kate said.
'It's time to talk.'